Whoops...
I'm Awesome

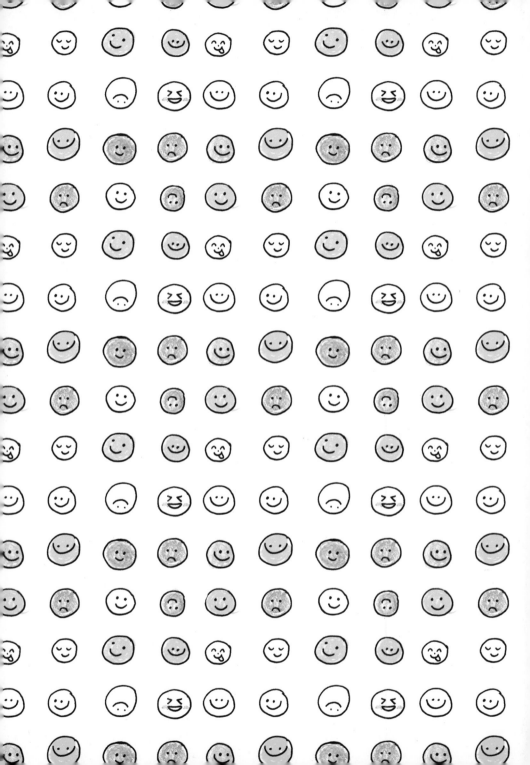

MELISSA VILLASEÑOR

Whoops...
I'm Awesome

A workbook with activities, art, and stories for embracing your wonderfully awesome self

CHRONICLE BOOKS
SAN FRANCISCO

Library of Congress Cataloging-in-Publication Data available.

ISBN 978-1-7972-1296-8

Manufactured in China.

Design by Lizzie Vaughan and Angie Kang.

Typesetting by Angie Kang. Typeset in Apercu and Gazpacho.

Author photograph by Robyn Von Swank.

America's Got Talent is a registered trademark of FremantleMedia North America Inc. Animal
Crossing, Mario Kart, Nintendo 64 are registered trademarks of Nintendo of America Inc. Aura
Cacia is a registered trademark of Frontier Distribution LLC. Best Friends Animal Society is a
registered trademark of Best Friends Animal Society. Bob's Red Mill is a registered trademark
of Bob's Red Mill Natural Foods. Cartoon Network is a registered trademark of The Cartoon
Network, Inc. Chase is a registered trademark of JP Morgan Chase Bank. Cream of Wheat is a
registered trademark of B&G Foods North America, Inc. Del Taco is a registered trademark of Del
Taco LLC. Etch A Sketch is a registered trademark of Spin Master LTD. *Family Guy* is a registered
trademark of Twentieth Century Fox Film Corporation. Goldeneye is a registered trademark of
Danjaq, LLC. Google is a registered trademark of Google LLC. Guinness is a registered trademark of Guinness & Co. Harvest Moon is a registered trademark of Natsume Inc. iMessage is a
registered trademark of Apple Inc. Insight Timer is a registered trademark of Insight Network
LLC. LEGO is a registered trademark of The LEGO Group. MAC is a registered trademark of
Estée Lauder Companies. Nike is a registered trademark of Nike Inc. Planned Parenthood is a
registered trademark of Planned Parenthood Federation of America, Inc. Play-Doh and Skip-It
are registered trademarks of Hasbro Inc. Polly Pocket is a registered trademark of Mattel Inc.
Rice Krispies is a registered trademark of Kellogg North America Company. *Saturday Night Live*
is a registered trademark of NBCUniversal Media, LLC. Silly Putty is a registered trademark of
Crayola Properties, Inc. Slinky is a registered trademark of James Industries, Inc. *South Park* is a
registered trademark of Comedy Partners Viacom International. StairMaster is a registered trademark of Core Health & Fitness LLC. Taco Bell is a registered trademark of Taco Bell. Tamogotchi
is a registered trademark of Kabushiki Kaisha Bandai (A.K.A. Bandai Co., Ltd.). Toyota Rav4 is a
registered trademark of Toyota Jidosha Kabushiki Taisha TA. TreePeople is a registered trademark
of TreePeople Land Trust. Vicks Vapo Rub is a registered trademark of The Procter & Gamble
Company. Wildwood Adventure Park is a registered trademark of Wildwood Estates, LLC.

10 9 8 7 6 5 4 3 2 1

Chronicle books and gifts are available at special quantity discounts to
corporations, professional associations, literacy programs, and other organizations.
For details and discount information, please contact our premiums department at
corporatesales@chroniclebooks.com or at 1-800-759-0190.

Chronicle Books LLC
680 Second Street
San Francisco, California 94107
www.chroniclebooks.com

I dedicate this book to my family.
Thank you for always making me laugh,
making me feel safe, and reminding
me who I am when I lose myself.

Introduction

Yo! Howdy! Welcome to my first journal! I'm Melissa Villaseñor! (Vee-uh-sen-your)

I would love to introduce myself in case you don't know much about me. I want you to get to know me better, but mainly, I want you to understand how I wandered into the land of making a journal with my art and interactive self-help activities.

On October 9, 1987—poof! I was born into a Mexican American family at a hospital in West Covina, California. I don't know the name of the hospital but I just know it was somewhere in West Covina. I was raised in Whittier, California. I am very close to my family, and my three siblings are my best friends.

Before I knew my gift of being a voice impressionist, I was very shy and let my older brother be in charge of stuff and do all the joking. I always loved being the kid who laughed at the other funny people, and I can see how that still is my favorite thing today. I really love when hilarious people make me laugh. When I was little I was a quiet one. I asked my mom recently, "Was I a cute kid? Did I have a lisp and stuff?" She said, "No, you didn't talk; it was creepy." But I think a lot of comedians are this way, just observing and writing it down.

By the time I hit the puberty chapter, I realized my obsession with pop singers in the early millennium, and I could impersonate my favorite singers (like Britney Spears, Christina Aguilera, Mandy Moore, and Shakira).

At my high school, Ramona Convent Secondary School in Alhambra, California, I shared my celebrity impressions with friends and received big laughs and amazed eyes. I finally did my high school talent show my sophomore year, and, not gonna lie, I crushed it. I knew from that moment what I was going to do with my life. It hit me like a lightning bolt.

I began doing stand-up comedy immediately after high school, making the forty-five-minute drive from Whittier to Hollywood to sign up for open mics. I shared my impressions in my act, and I got my first big break on NBC's *America's Got Talent,* Season 6. I have shared this funny story before: I was so upset to have to go audition for the show. A sweet lady whom I met from doing another TV show reached out to me on Facebook and said, "Hey! I am helping with *America's Got Talent* this year. You should audition—here's your appointment time." "Nooo," I thought to myself. "That show can really make a person look like a piece of shit if they bomb."

I dragged my feet and didn't even try hard at the first audition in LA. Sometimes, you guys, I can be so negative and have a "bad attitude," as my mom calls it. From that audition I got an email that said "Congrats! You are going to fly to Seattle and audition for the judges!" I thought, "NO, NO. PLEASE, NO." So I didn't expect much when I auditioned for the judges, who were at that time Sharon Osbourne, Piers Morgan, and Howie Mandel. However, it turned out to be one of my favorite moments ever! I received a theater full of laughs and, I believe, a standing ovation (no big deal, ha ha). I jumped for joy in my little heart and pranced off the stage feeling that I was a star. Boy, was that a lesson to not judge something right away. You never know the magic an opportunity can hold. From that moment, that first TV moment, I was known a bit more. Comedy clubs and colleges around the country were offering me weekends to headline shows—and get PAID for doing comedy. I was able to leave my part-time job at Forever 21 and be a touring comedian.

As I was on the road, I realized very quickly how bad I was at stand-up. I had only been doing ten- to fifteen-minute sets at shows in Los Angeles for about three years and wasn't nearly ready to headline. I went from ten minutes to needing to do forty minutes to an hour. That was hard shit. I was bombing on stage; I got laughs for the few impressions I had, but I crumbled inside my body up there in front of everyone. I remember many times going to my hotel room afterward and feeling hollow and angry with myself. I cried in so many hotels around the United States!

On top of that, I was heartbroken because a guy I was seeing at the time didn't want a relationship with me, yet I kept hanging on and hoping he would (classic twenty-four-year-old). So, of course, sadness arrived in my lap and I didn't know how to handle it. Thankfully, I expressed myself on paper and drew whatever I was feeling as I listened to sad music. To this day, I still love musicians who sing about something I'm going through—I feel I have a friend there with me.

I also love to sing, and I began writing songs on my ukulele and guitar. I've dipped my toes into many art forms because I get bored and emotional easily and need to express myself in different ways.

I've been on *Saturday Night Live* for six years now. That went by fast. The struggle I have with working

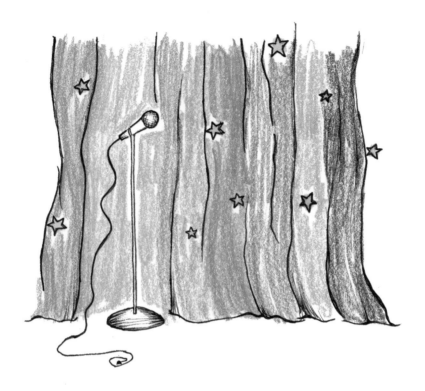

there is the feeling of not being enough. If I don't get to play and be a part of the show, it bruises my self-esteem. I take the form of me as I was as a kid. Shy, quiet, run to my room if I feel left out. And if that happens for weeks on end, it brings me down a hole and it takes me some time to get out and find the light. But even before *SNL*, my biggest struggle and the main thing I've worked on with my therapist has always been my self-esteem. So really, it isn't the show or anything external; it lies within me. I have a tough time getting out of the darkness and seriousness and into the light and silliness. Through the years, I have found specific things I run to that can help me get to the goofy me. She's my favorite me.

By my second year of *SNL*, I was going through a breakup, and I noticed that drawings were flowing out of me left and right. I began my art Instagram account @melissavart, sharing with my fans the side of me that can be real with emotions and not need the pressure to be funny. It's now a soothing place where I can feel safe and creative and connect with fans who share the same feelings and struggles.

After a few years of sharing my work, I gained fans solely for my art—it's so awesome! Some folks have even gotten tattoos of my drawings, and that's just a damn honor and warms my heart so much! The most common tattoo I've noticed folks getting is my self-love arms.

As I began selling prints and T-shirts with my art, many folks asked, "OK, Meliss', when will you have a book out?!" and I thought, "HEY! You're right! I GOTTA MAKE A BOOK!!"

I asked myself, All right, well, what do I want to share? What books am I personally always drawn to? What is Melissa's ideal book to soak into? My answer? I always enjoy books that remind me I'm not alone, books where I don't have to do a lot of reading (I struggle with reading comprehension) and can just look at drawings and do some interactive activities. Books like Shel Silverstein's where there are little sayings and drawings that are simple and cute, yet hold something deep and meaningful. Books that say it's very OK to be flawed and filled with mistakes but keep going by pushing away the seriousness that gets in the way of living that Silly Putty life.

I love books that have a lot of heart and humor and stories. I love journals that celebrate all the sides of you, the dark and the light, and allowing the mess. The beautiful, wild, sensitive mess. So that is what I want to share with you!

I hope that this journal, and all I've learned so far from the self-care and spiritual books and experiences that have shaped me, helps you as much as it's helped me.

Fuck 'em.
I'm my favorite.

Whenever I step out of myself and take a good look at my comedy, music, and drawings, I notice a common thread: Being my own best friend, sharing my truth, and making myself laugh. When I do stand-up, I just aim to make myself laugh (usually with the dumbest things), and I heal myself and hope the audience heals and laughs too. Because everyone is in pain for some reason or another. So! Let's do this. Let's become best buds with ourselves.

With this journal, I asked myself, What do I, Melissa, do to get to that silly place? How oh how do I get there? Throughout these pages, I'll share what your pal Meliss' does. I wanna help you:

1. **Embrace Your Kid Mind**
   *music, new adventures, art, cartoons,
   nostalgic stuff*

2. **Get Your Body Moving**
   *exercising, walking with your dog, hanging
   with nature*

3. **Care for Your Mind, Spirit, and Soul**
   *meditation, affirmations, visualization,
   home, photos*

4. **Do Good and Help Others**
   *volunteering, taking care of the environment,
   listening*

Embrace Your Kid Mind

Embracing my childlike mind helps me get back to myself.

Whenever adult pressures of work and seriousness are too much, I try to stop and make some time to get back in touch with the little Melissa within.

When I feel jealous or competitive and worried and not in control of things, that's the time to step out of that and plop into some simple relaxing hobby, or simply do nothing. I remember as a kid sometimes just doing nothing but pickin' my nose, and that was enough fun for the day. One time I was on the road doing stand-up and was alone in my hotel room. I was picking my belly button and pulled out a tiny rock of lint that had piled up from the years. It made me laugh so much. I saved it too. Ha ha, just kidding.

For me, nothing great comes out of that place of worry and control. I create my best ideas when I'm calm and free. I'm kinder too.

There are so many things out there to distract us and make us forget who we are and what we truly want for ourselves. Our wires get so tangled with others that we forget who we are.

What are some things little kid you would be so proud of that you've accomplished as an adult?

HERE ARE SOME THINGS LITTLE

MELISSA WOULD BE PROUD OF:

1. I can tie my shoes and make a living!

2. I made it on my dream show, and I made a music album with my own songs.

3. I'm happy with my appearance and my body (I used to be embarrassed by my freckles, the sweat drops that start on my nose, and my thick fluffy hair that broke every rubber band in sight).

4. I own colorful clothes that I mix and match, and I own my own makeup. (As a kid, I loved throwing tons of necklaces, purses—really anything on me wherever I went.)

5. I can cook! (well, good breakfasts mainly)

Here are some things little

_____ would be proud of:

(your name)

_____

_____

_____

_____

_____

_____

_____

_____

_____

_____

_____

For all the ones
who played a
tree, you're a
star to me.

Childhood Toys

Write a list of your favorite toys as a kid. I'll go first!

SLINKY

I first had a plastic rainbow star one that was so pretty and mesmerizing. But then my funny cousin, who just was too strong for her own good, came over one time and bent it up and tangled it. Then my dad tried to fix it and tried to make me believe it was fixed, when really, it had a gap in it that I could not look away from.

SKIP-IT

Skip-It was this ankle toy that would swing around one ankle while the other foot jumped over it.

POLLY POCKET

The '90s Polly Pocket was just the best. The colors were pink and pretty, and Polly was so cute in her tiny little world. I just loved it when there was a little bridge inside the case.

PLAY-DOH

I've always loved the smell of Play-Doh, and the taste is kind of salty. Don't worry, I don't lick it . . . often.

VIDEO GAMES

My brother got an N64 one Christmas and it was the first video game system we had in our house. It was so cool and I eventually would play when he got more controllers and multiplayer games like *Mario Kart*, *007 Goldeneye*, and *Harvest Moon*. I always enjoyed when I could just walk around a town and swim. So, obviously, today *Animal Crossing* is my favorite game. It's just a game where you take care of a town and mail letters to neighbors and help keep the town clean and cute.

WHOOPEE CUSHIONS

Well, obviously, farts will always be funny. I don't need whoopee cushions today because, well, I'm tootin' all the time.

VIRTUAL PETS

Ahhh, I had a few different virtual pets—Tamagotchi, Nano Kitty, and some other ones too.

ETCH A SKETCH

I loved writing on something and making it disappear. I think I got an Etch A Sketch because I enjoyed watching my teacher write on the marker board and then wipe it off. At home I would pretend I was a teacher wiping off my Etch A Sketch.

Now you make your list of
your favorite toys as a kid!

_____

_____

_____

_____

_____

_____

_____

_____

_____

_____

_____

Other things to get back to being myself (and maybe yourself too)

Obviously, I don't play with a lot of those kid toys as an adult. But here are some things I can do as an adult to help me get back to me.

LISTEN TO MUSIC

Listen to '90s pop—I'm talking NSYNC and some early millennium tunes—good ole Nickelback and Creed. They really make me smile and laugh, but most importantly, they empower me. I love rusty, weathered voices that say, "I've been bruised and broken, but I'm getting back up and not giving up!" What's that U2 song that goes something like, "You've got to get yourself together, you've got stuck in a moment and now you can't get out of it"? Oh, right, "Stuck in a Moment You Can't Get Out Of"! Duh. I love that stuff. Corny but inspiring.

Oh, and Dolly Parton. Fill yourself with Dolly. Just trust me, any direction of Dolly you go in, it'll only bring you to happy. I fell in love with Dolly in the summer of 2020. I was listening to her songs and wanted to dive deeper, so I found the audiobook *Dream More*. Her words and voice and a cappella singing made me feel I had a friend right there with me.

FOOD

Eat your favorite childhood foods as a treat for you. What's your favorite cereal? Mine was Rice Krispies. I love the pop sounds it makes when the milk gets poured in there. Favorite dessert? Mine is a classic Funfetti cake . . . oooh, or cookie dough ice cream! Spaghetti and mac 'n' cheese always make me feel like me and a bean and cheese burrito too. When I was little, my siblings and I would just order plain bean and cheese burritos (no chili, no red sauce) from Taco Bell. Unfortunately, I can't have Taco Bell that much these days because . . . you know. I'd have to cancel my next-day schedule and just hang with Mr. Toilet.

FRIENDS

The pals that light you up. Lift you up. Those are the pals. If anyone makes you feel less than or anxious, weed them out. You don't deserve that or have time for it. Sometimes you can grow out of friendships, and that's OK. One changes and one doesn't, and that's just how it goes. It's life. I had a dear friend in high school, Sindie, but after, for about ten years, we hardly spoke. But then, just at the right time, when both of us had grown, we were sewn back into each other's lives. She is one of my best friends today. I love when I can simply think of Sindie and smile and feel calm. Those are amazing people and the ones to hold close, the ones who make you breathe calmly. I wonder if I am that for anyone in my life—I feel I can be, but I can also be a real party pooper. I mean, if you take me on a vacation, I'm not one to do every sightseeing event; if I see a nice chair in the lobby, I kinda wanna plant myself there for a bit. Just a warning.

FAMILY

My family reminds me of who I am whenever I start to drift off into the clouds of ego. I am a bit of an empath and a sponge (impressionist), so I can soak in others and forget myself. I run to my sister, Allie, when I start to float. I go to her because she is this strong, funny, adorable person, and we laugh together and just get each other. My brothers too.

Michael is so funny and intelligent, and I love picking his brain. He is so well versed in the news, and I always need someone to break it down for me in Melissa-brain form. My brother Andrew is super funny too. He is probably the most naturally funny sibling. He doesn't have to try, and the way he delivers words is hysterical. Gosh, the Villaseñors are a funny bunch!

DRAW

Obviously, this is a childlike thing that I have grown and gotten better at. It's a place where I get quiet, reflective, cathartic, and peaceful. I release what I'm feeling when I draw. I get lost in the world that appears on the paper.

Now you try!
Don't overthink it, just draw.

TRY SOMETHING NEW

As a kid, the world was new and amazing. We don't know everything, even as adults, so there's always something cool to learn or try—sometimes without any goal of perfection or being pro.

CARTOONS

What can be more childlike than cartoons? I like when I
turn on the TV and see *South Park* or *Family Guy* on. It takes
me out of the human world and into colorful animation.
I do a bit of voiceover for cartoons these days, and boy, it's
a blast. It can turn my day around. I can be in a gloomy
mood, but the minute I walk into a recording studio and
voice a feisty raccoon or a jolly fish, well, I've got no choice
but to laugh and smile. Every time I walk out of a voiceover
booth, I always feel happy and honestly grateful that I can
do this as my job.

Write the lines that this little squirrel would say in this comic strip . . .

NO PLAN

Plan a "no-plan" day, where you don't have a schedule—
you just float like a leaf in the wind, he-he. It's a great
thing for you.

For example, one Sunday, I was with my family and told
them, "You guys do what you want, and I will follow and not
complain, I promise." "Sure," my mom says, "yeah, right!"
(Ha ha, I've been a complainer as a kid on many family trips.)
On one of these "do what you want" days, we went to the
beach and got buried in the sand. I had never had that
happen to me before and it really "GROUNDED" me. Another
time, I was trying really hard to fix my water hose, but it
wasn't tightened enough and (splash!) water squirted right in
my face. You bet I gave a hilarious ugly scream; that's what I
do when I get shocked. It sounds like "OIGHHHHGG!"

The no-plan day is usually a good plan.

Whoops . . . I'm Awesome

Write in the Heart

Write in this heart the tiniest, simplest things that bring you joy: A new journal! Sunlight on your face! Yarn! We forget how those little things can make a huge difference.

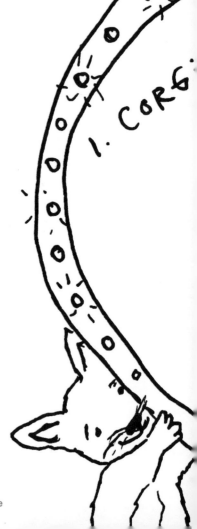

1. CORG

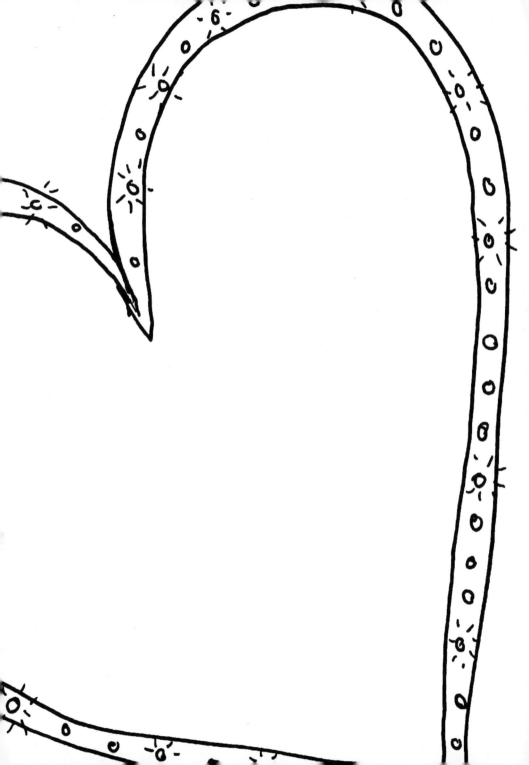

Oh man, something I love more and more . . . a BATH! A BUBBLE BATH!

I enjoy sitting in a bubble bath and moving the bubbles around. Why are bubbles so pretty and soothing? I think it's because bubbles are a metaphor for thoughts. They can just float, pop, and disappear. One time, I was feelin' crappy poo, and I made myself a nice bubble bath and put bubbles on my face and pretended I was Santa Claus for a bit. I soon was laughing again.

Snails (and You) Are Awesome!

View each day like a kid, always learning because there is always something new to learn! I learned recently, at thirty-four years old, that snails leave that glittery line of goo you see on sidewalks. I just thought someone dropped glitter by accident. But no! It's the lil' snails! (Also, a warning: don't google "snail trail" unless you like nasty stuff.)

I love learning fun facts. I love sharing how to spot poison ivy when I go hiking with a friend. I shout, "LEAVES OF THREE, LET THEM BE!" and my friend usually says, "OK, calm down."

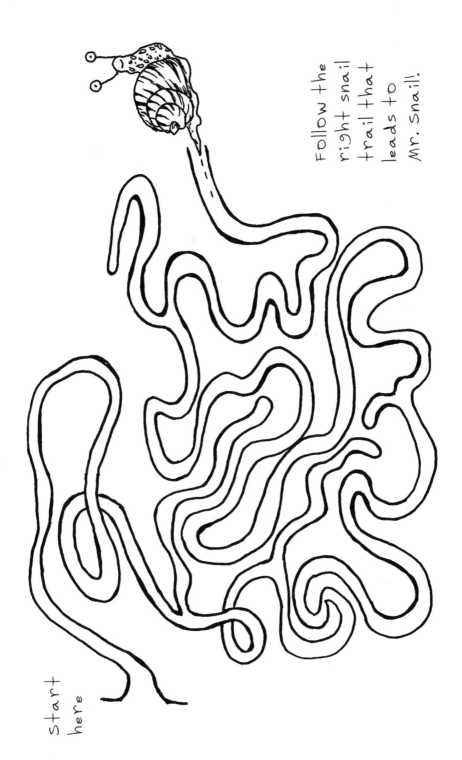

Follow the right snail trail that leads to Mr. Snail!

start here

Cloud-Spotting

This looks like a slipper
(or if you grew up in a
Mexican household, a
"chancla")!

Oooh! An arrow?
Mushroom! Tree! Lamp!

Whoa! A confident
bird leaping into
the sky.

A very fancy poodle!

Take some time to stare at some clouds.
Take this with you, and draw the clouds you see
here. What do you think they look like?
Now it's your turn!!! Go!

Bird-Watching

Do you have binoculars? If not, get some! It's fun to bird-watch. I took up this hobby in my early twenties. You can usually find bird-watching groups in your city through the Audubon Society.

Do you have a favorite bird? A bluebird? Maybe a peacock? If you were a bird, what kind would you be? (I started the feet for you.)

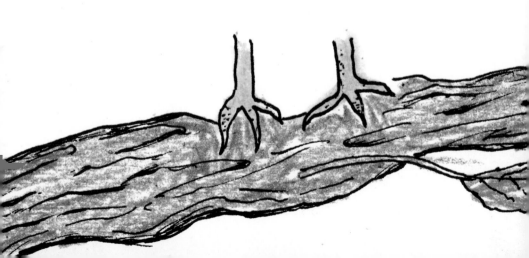

Get Your Body Moving

First, before we go any further, pat yourself on the back or shoulder, because, damn, you're alive! Congrats.

A key ingredient to being awesome is being awesome to your body. In order to do good, joyful things out there in the world, ya gotta start right here, with you. Sometimes I sit around and wonder, "Why do I feel so blue?" and I realize, "Oh, it's probably because I haven't taken in any nature today; I haven't gotten outside air and moved my body." So yes, this chapter is all about exercise and movement to get out of our brains that question so much. I find it's important to take some time out of the day to give myself a workout, a walk in the park, any kind of movement—it goes a long way.

One of the best things that came out of my twenties was that I started to exercise.

Whenever I slump around, mentally or physically, I know it means I need to move. Get up. Even if it's just for a walk, WALK. I like the sweat—I feel accomplished and super pumped after I run or do Pilates.

Ohh! Wanna know something cool? I actually have recurring (just learned it's "recurring," not "reoccuring") dreams where I run so fast that I begin to take off and fly into the sky. Isn't that cool?

I try to work out every other day, if possible, and change up the workouts. I believe if you do the same workout every time, like anything, your body gets used to it and your brain gets bored. It's all about changing it up and having fun.

I actually want to take a movement/dance class next because I'm a bit stiff and probably the worst Latina dancer on the planet. It sucks, ha ha.

Sometimes I'll just stay in my apartment and do different YouTube workouts (thanks to the ladies at PopSugar for their great uploads). I love this one forty-five-minute Pilates workout—I get so sore from it and also get so annoyed at hearing them say, "Oooh, I feel that burn! Pretend you're making guacamole with this movement. Gosh, now I want some guacamole, bhahahah!" It is such a good workout that every time, I have to pause it to breathe and say, "Oh, you son of a bitch," 'cause she's workin' me hard (but I'm having fun!?).

Like anything new, it's great to start small, then add on. I used to run for twenty minutes. I keep adding more time, and then my body gets used to it.

Funny fact: In August 2021, I was invited to do the New York Marathon, the 26-mile [42 km] one, and I said yes! But then my family laughed at me for this and I got defensive and said, "WHAT'S SO FUNNY?" They had a good point, that a 26-mile marathon is a huge thing to prep for and I could get seriously injured, BUT I do want to train for a future marathon and I can and I will. I ended up going to the marathon that year and handed out medals at the finish line. It felt good to be a part of it all!

Pro tip: It's important to have great posture when running—no slumping! I know we are so used to the Gollum body shape (thanks, phones), but stand up straight! You'll feel more confident and beautiful too.

Whoops . . . I'm Awesome

Exercise Inspiration

Sometimes there are days where I just want to do something easy and tone my bod. Thanks to good ol' Google, I look up what I want to tone—I'll type in "arm workout," "booty workout," or "ab workout," and these fun little images of a cartoony body appear and show me how to do it. It's amazing that we can have such quick access to these! So here, as your own personal Google, I have drawn out some of my favorite toning workouts that require no weights, no fancy equipment, just you. The only thing I suggest you have is one of those workout or yoga mats. And put some fun music on too. If you need any tips, I've included a playlist of songs I like to work out to.

Warning: Before you look at these drawings of a person (me) working out . . . I drew these on a day where I was giving up hope on myself. Sure they may look a little crappy, but at least I still did it, and that's a win for me!

If you like these examples, there are so many more online! Just look them up.

Booty!!

BRIDGE

10 reps, hold for 7 seconds each

DONKEY KICK

30 on each leg, 3 sets

SUMO SQUAT

20 reps

FIRE HYDRANT

30 on each leg, 3 sets

WALL SIT

Hold for 1 minute

Guess what?
Chicken butt!

Dumbbell
weights (they
aren't that
dumb)

Water
(agua)

Ankle weights
(not burgers)

(Not a purse)
Eh, if I see
this thing,
I'll use it for
sumo squats.

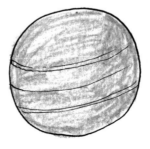

Ball (Good for
ab stuff or
just bouncing
around)

Buff Arms!

I use 5 or 3 lb weights, but use whatever works for you.
I like to do 2 to 3 sets with 15 reps for each exercise.

FLY BIRD

WITH ARMS WIDE OPEN!

FRONT LIFT

TRICEP KICKBACKS

RAISE THE ROOF!

TRICEP DIPS

Here is my workout playlist:

"Be Good to Yourself"
Journey

"What I Got"
Sublime

"I Don't Feel Like Dancin'"
Scissor Sisters

"Juice"
Lizzo

"Ain't It Fun"
Paramore

"Higher Love"
Kygo and Whitney Houston

"Levitating"
Dua Lipa

"Bad Decisions"
The Strokes

"I'm Coming Out"
Diana Ross

"One Life, Might Live"
Little Simz

"Go the Distance"
Hercules Original Soundtrack (or really anything from this album)

"Real World"
Matchbox Twenty

"The Tide Is High"
Blondie

"Livin' Thing"
ELO

"Peace of Mind"
Boston

"True to Your Heart"
98 Degrees and Stevie Wonder

"Rich Girl"
Hall & Oates

Dog Walk

If you have a doggie, you already know the wonders of
simply walking outside. If you don't have a dog, take
yourself on a walk. It's one of the best forms of meditation
and relaxation. You'll notice more things on the street,
and it really helps your mind calm down and even get
creative ideas. Sometimes I jog with my dog, Penny, and
we both smile in the sun and get filled with endorphins
(happy chemicals).

On your next walk, let your mind wander.
What did you think about? Jot it down here
to capture the moments.

_____

_____

_____

_____

_____

_____

_____

_____

_____

_____

Hiking

Hiking, oh I love to hike. Now, I don't do lots of extreme hiking with the steep, steep hills. Sometimes my asthma catches up with me and I feel a little wheezy.

I don't know where you are located, but I hope there are hiking trails or at least some nice big park trails to walk on. If I'm in New York, I'll try to go to a park in the city or upstate to the Catskills because they have such pretty hikes there. If I'm in LA, I go to hiking trails outside of the fluffy Hollywood town because, ehh, I don't like it when it's too packed. And being freakin' famous I don't want to get noticed all the time. Ha ha ha, just kidding, I love it! I love when people say, "Yo, Meliss'! Big fan!" It makes my whole day, and it's a reminder I am bringing joy. It's an honor that I can help folks feel good and smile.

It makes me so happy when I fly into states and towns that have secluded trails for people to walk or bike on because it's just so needed for humanity. I love it when cities add nature back to the land with trees and flowers and brush. (I don't think "brush" is the right word; I mean "bushes"? "Brushies"?) City life all the time is just not healthy. It takes us away from our connection to the earth.

Which path leads to the tippy top?

(psst, sometimes there's more than one way to get to the tippy top)

START

Something Different

Sometimes I take a walk outside, and it's usually the same ol' walk. Turn here, then here, then right at the Del Taco, then left at the Chase bank, and back home. It becomes boring. So, go in a different direction one day! Or walk forward, then back a few times—pretend you're Willy Wonka. Maybe attempt a cartwheel at a park or a roly-poly (if you can't cartwheel). If you can't do a roly-poly, at least do a worm movement on the ground. Walk backward—I bet that'll make you smile. Doing a little bit of different can make a nice change. Recently, I tried to roll down the hill of my parents' front yard! Welp—it made me dizzy as hell. Some things don't work that great in your thirties. When I was eight years old, I could do that no problem. Note to self: Don't do that in my eighties or my head will fly off.

> One time I was on the road for a stand-up tour and felt I needed some adventure, so I found a place called Wildwood Adventure Park in Manhattan, Kansas, which has seven different ziplines. I did all of them! I flew high above a forest! It was so fun!

Whoops . . . I'm Awesome

If you could go walking around anywhere (seriously, anywhere), where would it be? Who would you want to come with you on a walk? What would you want to talk about?

_____

_____

_____

_____

_____

_____

_____

_____

_____

_____

Nap Love

If you can nap, do it. I love naps AND I'M NOT ASHAMED
TO SAY IT!

I am someone who needs them because I do stand-up
shows at night and am often on the road somewhere. I need
to regain energy for the stage, especially if the day requires
traveling and flights. I also take naps to be quiet and not smile
because I speak, sing, and smile so damn much on stage.

I think an hour nap or less is good. I like that naps speed
up the day, especially if you aren't a fan of the day you're
having. They can also get you in a better mood. Sometimes
I wake up in the morning like a grump, and a nap around
1 p.m. or 3 p.m. can make me a happy baby, as I like to say.

"I'm always down to nap"
means: I'm down to shut
this world, my voice, and
my thoughts up. This day
is too much and I need
a pause/restart. This
energy better be gone by
the time I wake up.

THE "DO YOU NEED A NAP?" QUIZ!

Question 1:
Are your eyes feeling heavy?

A. naw
B. yessss
C. That's just my face.

Question 2:
How's your mood?
Are you a grumpy dumpy?

A. How dare you.
B. You know what? Yeah, I sure am a grump.
C. No, seriously, that's just my face.

Question 3:
Are you lacking the energy
right now to keep working?

A. Yeah, but I need to keep plowing through.
B. Sure, I feel like a snail.
C. I don't know.

Question 4:
Do you like power naps?

A. Not really.
B. Yes, I notice it does give me an extra energy boost.
C. I mean, yeah, but I never really feel the "power."

Question 5:
Are you afraid to admit that you are a nap queen/king?

A. Yes, I don't want people to think I'm an old fart.
B. Hell naw. Proud of it!
C. Shut up.

Question 6:
Do you notice that you get creative ideas after a nap?

A. I've never paid attention to that.
B. Oh yeah! I got an idea to draw a tongue licking an eyeball lollipop!
C. I am not creative. And I don't got time.

Question 7:
Do you notice that you are filled with more joy after sleep?

A. Umm, maybe, yeah.
B. Hot diggity dog I am! I want to skip around town.
C. Joy is for Marie Kondo only.

Question 8:
Are you thinking about your pillow and blanket right now?

A. No, that's weird.
B. Ha ha, yeah, actually I am!
C. I don't use pillows or blankets.

If you answered . . . Mostly A's: You need a hug and a nap! Mostly B's: I love that you love naps! Go for it. Mostly C's: You are hilarious and I hope you can let your guard down and find the softness—and find time to nap it up!

soften.

How Do You Sleep?

I sleep on my side, but for most of my kid and teen years, I actually slept on my belly. Which made me think at one point that was the reason why my boobies never grew, because I smashed them as I slept. So dumb.

If you sleep on your back, that's amazing and creepy. I think my grandma sleeps with her hands in prayer position.

How many pillows do you use? I like a good three. The main one in the middle and two on the sides for me to hug when I switch sides while sleeping.

Unfortunately, I'm not a fan of spooning. I can't handle someone breathing on me; it's distracting, smelly, and creepy. I can't spoon another person because that one arm goes numb, so forget it. I am happy to spoon for a solid minute, but that's it.

THE "SHUT UP WORLD"

Where you've just had it with everything.

THE "SIDE WITH PILLOW FRIEND"

The only spooning you can do without your arm going numb.

THE "MUMMY CASKET/SLEEPING BEAUTY"

But don't kiss because breath stinks.

In the winter, my doggie, Penny,
sleeps curled up in a croissant
shape under my blankets, and
she's like this little heater that
makes me feel safe and warm.
It's the best best!

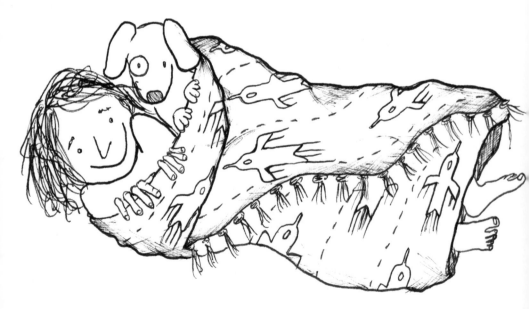

sniff sniff.

Smelly Smells

Which smells give you comfort?

I use essential oils to get to the heart of a really good smell. I use a few for different occasions—I love peppermint for when I get headaches or need to wake up. You can place a little drop or two on your temples on the sides of your head. I like lavender on my pillow when I sleep and geranium as a soothing smell during the day. Just place any of them on your wrist and take a whiff. I enjoy the Aura Cacia brand of essential oils, but get whatever ones work for you—some can get pricey and it's like, ehhh, come on, man, I don't wanna spend 60 bucks on a couple of drops.

I don't know if this is an "official" essential oil, but I grew up on Vicks VapoRub and still use it to this day when I sleep—it helps me breathe well and is nostalgic, but mainly it's great if I catch a cold. I've noticed a lot Mexican families have a common routine of placing some VapoRub on the neck and chest and the bottoms of the feet when you're sick. I don't know why, but trust me—it works. I'll be straight with you, I would love if the Indiana Jones ride at Disneyland made a candle with that smell that's in there! It's like a musky mildew-y treasure.

What do you like to sniff? How does it make you feel? Is there a smell memory you wish came in a scented candle or was distilled into an essential oil?

_____

_____

_____

_____

_____

_____

_____

_____

_____

Food

I try to follow a healthy lifestyle, but of course I sprinkle some treats in the mix 'cause I freakin' deserve it. Thank goodness I've grown to enjoy healthy foods. When I was a kid, boy, was I one picky eater. I grew up with homemade meals (lotta Mexican food, which I didn't like as a kid because we had it all the time; now it's my favorite). I didn't like french fries (who doesn't like french fries??); I didn't like strawberries because of the sensation of the tiny seeds; and I didn't like any vegetables. Man, I was a pain in the ass. I was content with eating oatmeal, though, and I would request *avena* (which is Spanish for *oatmeal*) all the time, which IS healthy.

By my second year on SNL, I began to get obsessed with how I looked on TV so I stopped eating a lot of food—I remember just having nuts for a meal. That's NUTS. I ate "healthy" (no cheese, no dairy, no alcohol, no bread); I cut out a lot, and my body got super thin and weak. I felt dizzy and faint, and that things were going in slow motion—it wasn't healthy. My hair began to fall out, and my bones would ache from the tiniest of workouts. I'm glad I got out of that harmful obsession because it could have gotten scary if I stuck with it much longer.

Now, I listen to my body. I eat what I'm craving. I can tell when I've eaten too much junk because my body feels awful, and I don't have energy. I'm not used to high-sodium food, and if I eat too much sodium, I get dizzy and weird (and not the good kind of weird). So, it's about balance for me.

Today, I love bananas and apples! Blueberries and strawberries! I love spinach and avocado and broccoli! When I moved to the Hollywood area, I learned what kombucha and quinoa were. I like lentil pasta! I do! Most folks don't and that's fine, I ain't gonna push it on you. Ha ha ha, but I love it. It's a good source of protein, just throw on a lot of olive oil, ya goof!

I didn't start seeing the results of my workouts until I stopped drinking alcohol and devouring sugary cereal and mac 'n' cheese at midnight. Ha ha, "mac 'n' cheese at midnight" sounds like a sexy jam. My favorite beer was Guinness, RIP, and my favorite cereal was Frosted Mini-Wheats. I'd let those minis soak up all the 2% milk. Oh yeah, by the way, I was drinking a lot of 2% milk up until my mid-twenties. Now it's all about that almond and oat milk, baby.

I rarely drink alcohol, but when I do, it's a special occasion. A glass of wine with my pasta is nice. I don't know much about the alcohol world, and I don't really care to find out. But sometimes a little drink can help me get out of my serious intense Melissa mode.

The main thing I'm working on when it comes to eating these days is chewing more slowly and enjoying my meals. I don't want to eat like a crazy raccoon anymore! I've learned that it takes about twenty minutes for our brains to signal we are full. So sometimes we continuously eat for twenty minutes and are so stuffed we can't think or talk to anyone. The only thing we may be able to say is, "Pop, I might pop."

Me after eating
my food too fast.

WORD SEARCH TIME!

Can you find and circle all these foods the raccoon (me) ate?

Almonds	Beans	Bread
Cheese	Chips	*(oh whoops, I think rice isn't in there.)
Pizza	Avocado	
Apple	Eggs	
Rice*	Potato	

A	Z	Z	i	P	B	E	A	N	S
L	Q	A	V	O	C	A	D	O	G
M	F	E	T	T	M	P	A	B	C
O	L	G	Q	A	S	P	E	V	R
N	Z	G	I	T	S	L	R	S	Z
D	N	S	M	O	H	E	B	P	W
S	P	i	H	C	H	E	E	S	E

Some Melissa Recipes

CHOCOLATE PROTEIN SPINACH BANANA SMOOTHIE

I enjoy this smoothie, which I make often in the morning. Yes, I stole the recipe from a popular juice shop in New York. Look, if you see the ingredients on the menu, have the time, and own a juice blender? Don't waste your money on that thang.

Feel free to make this recipe your own; the ingredients are measured really, really casually, so add or omit whatever you'd like.

A dollop of yogurt

A splash of almond milk

1 scoop chocolate whey protein

1 banana

Handful of spinach

1/2 tsp almond butter (or however much you want, pal)

Granola (optional)

Goji berries (optional)

Put the first six ingredients in a blender and mix it up. Put it in the fridge; it's so yummy a bit colder. Maybe wait an hour? Or make it the night before so it's cold in the morning. Then, when you're going to dive into it, top it with granola and some goji berries (yeah, I know, those things can be pricey, so no pressure).

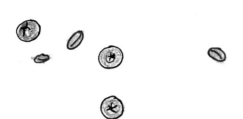

Fun fact! Sometimes at night when I can't decide what to eat, I'll eat oatmeal!

OATMEAL

I like the Bob's Red Mill oatmeal brand. Maybe I trust Bob? I love oatmeal because you can put so many yummy toppings on it. I usually make two servings because I want extra to save in the fridge for the next day.

1 cup [100 g] rolled oats

A sprinkle of cinnamon (if you want to feel like Christmas)

Flax seeds (huge source of fiber and they don't taste like anything!)

Chia seeds (same as above)

SOME MORE TOPPINGS INSPIRATION:

Dab of almond butter

Handful of blueberries

1/2 banana, sliced

Handful of walnuts and/or pepitas

In a medium saucepan over high heat, bring 2 cups [480 ml] of water to a boil. Turn the heat to low and let it simmer for a couple of minutes. Once the oats are soft, spoon them into a bowl and top with the cinnamon, flax seeds, and chia seeds, and any other toppings of your choice. Mmmm! Enjoy!

BEAN 'N' CHEESE BURRITO

I make a lot of bean and cheese burritos at home. I can tell when my body is lacking frijoles. They are a great source of iron and make me feel strong.

Add whatever you enjoy to it!

Throw a can of black beans in a large pot and heat them up. On a big pan, warm up a wheat tortilla. Then put that tortilla on a plate, put some beans on there, and top it with cheese (I do vegan) and sliced avocado. If it's breakfast, add some scrambled eggs to that sucker.

Side note: I love when my parents pick me up from the airport after a long day of travels and they have a great big burrito ready for me (which is almost always). A burrito after a day of traveling is the best.

Comfort Foods

There are many nights when I don't know what to eat or what I'm craving. Sometimes it's quite late at night, but I know I need to eat something, and that's when I whip out the Cream of Wheat. It's very comforting, filling, and healthy (lots of iron!). I was brought up with Cream of Wheat at night. It's something my mom did with us as kids. I got the love for it from her. To this day, if I am unsure about what to eat, have no fear, Cream of Wheat is here!

What is a go-to comfort food recipe that makes you feel super healthy and powerful, inside and out? Why? What are some foods you didn't like as a kid but you do now? Also, it's okay if you don't know why.

_____

_____

_____

_____

_____

_____

_____

_____

_____

_____

Care for Your Mind, Spirit, and Soul

our brains are a circus, huh?

We can have so many ridiculous, mean thoughts about ourselves and others flying through our heads, and it does no good! I know I can really spiral and start to agree with those pesky thoughts if I stay in my head too long. But thankfully, there are some good tools out there that can help quiet those fools.

Every now and
then, come back
down to Earth.

Write some affirmations!

In my twenties, I was introduced to some new cool things, and I'm not talkin' about crying for dudes who didn't want me and Guinness beer and a septum piercing (which didn't work for me; you have to have a cute button nose for that, and mine ain't)! I'm talkin' about the self-care things I started to dip my toes into, like meditation, affirmations, law of attraction, gratitude lists, and morning pages. So, let's get into it!

Affirmations

Jack Canfield, one of my favorite motivational speakers/ authors, said about daily affirmations: "Daily affirmations are clear, positive statements that describe your goals as already achieved."

For a long time, my goals and dreams were all in my head. I never said them out loud, especially to others, because I felt that'd be silly—like I'd jinx it somehow. Trust me, though, there is so much power in saying them out loud and visualizing the dreams coming true and taking action at working at them daily.

Adding affirmations to my daily routine helped me get to that stronger Melissa. You can say them whenever you want! Ideally, I like to say them in the morning, but you can scatter them throughout the day. I say them out loud when I'm driving or walking on the street or in the shower. Yes, obviously I whisper them

if someone walks right by me. I don't want them to call the cops because I'm repeating, "I am a really talented person! I'm hilarious!"

I started going to therapy when I was twenty-six. I wanted to work on my self-esteem and belief in myself. My first therapist, also named Melissa (I felt that was a good sign), worked in my hometown of Whittier, and she helped me find my strength. She sent me home with CDs of Jack Canfield's *The Success Principles*. I began listening to them in my 2008 Toyota RAV4 (which I still have today, hell yeah). I would drive around LA listening, and I began to fall in love with these awesome words and teachings. He is funny and inspiring, and makes sense to my brain! He shares so much on how you can get what you want in life, but the thing that really stuck with me is the affirmations routine. He suggests you write each of your dreams on a notecard and say it out loud, in the morning and before bed. Act as though it's already true; close your eyes and visualize it happening (hear it too). Then when it does come true, you can get rid of that card and add new ones. I'm telling you, this is how I got *SNL*. In 2016, every morning I'd close my eyes and see myself in the intro credits of the show, and later that year, I was on the show. It's very powerful. On the left page are my latest affirmations on sticky notes that you can use as a jumping off point. Oh, and you don't need to worry about the how or when or where; it's on the way.

Now you try!

Write down some things you want for yourself. It could be anything, but it's best to be specific and NOT SILLY. Do not judge it. What would you want without letting fear take over? Maybe it's an ideal body weight, a vacation you want to take by a particular month of the year, a new job where you utilize your talents and passion.

In the spring of 2016, I was inspired by this actress I met and worked with named Kali Hawk. I met her on this voiceover recording for a cartoon called *OK K.O.! Let's Be Heroes* that was on Cartoon Network. After our recording session, we went to have pizza at this place in Burbank. We sat down at the red-and-white checkered table, and as the first bite of pizza stung my gums, Kali Hawk was sharing her journey. I was listening quietly and was amazed by her successful career. Kali said, "I just ask the universe for what I want and I get it." I thought, "OK, loony," but I started trying that out, and honestly, it builds up your belief in yourself (and also, hearing yourself can be powerful). Later, I began asking the universe for anything I wanted: "Dear universe, I would like a wonderful man in my life." "Yo, universe! I want a Spanish-style home at some point in my thirties!" "Hey, hey, universe, I'd love to be busy with jobs like voiceover cartoons, acting roles, and stand-up shows." Sometimes when I feel stressed while working on *SNL*, I simply close my eyes and ask, "Angels, please help me use my talents to bring laughs, create joy, and heal folks. Help guide me to work hard and fill me with great ideas." We can't do this stuff alone, guys. We all need help.

And yes, of course some days it's freakin' hard to say them when you feel like a crumbled cookie.

On those days, I just let go a bit and accept my crumbles and take care of me. It'll pass. It'll pass.

But hey—
some of the
sweetest
things crumble!

Meditation

Some meditation teachers I adore are Jack Kornfield
(yes, different from Jack Canfield), Tara Brach, and Sarah
Blondin. They have soothing voices and you can find their
guided meditations online for free! I enjoy this meditation
app called Insight Timer. It's filled with meditations and music.

This drawing was inspired by a Jack Kornfield meditation
called "Big Mind Meditation." He talks about how our brains
are like the sky, and thoughts come and go like clouds.

Ommmm!!

Some days meditation brings me some creative ideas, and some days it doesn't. Regardless, I do notice it helps me not react so quickly to things that upset me.

For the folks who can't sit and meditate, don't worry. There are lots of different forms of meditation. For example, my mom could never sit and meditate. Her meditation is cleaning and watering the plants. When I was a kid, I remember being inside the house watching cartoons and seeing her outside with the hose just watering and finding peace. I'd be thinking, "Why the heck does she do that work so much?" Well, because that's what gets her to that quiet place.

Fun story: I would drink from the water hose all the time as a kid and one time it was connected to our fish pond and I straight-up drank algae water. Maybe that's what made me loca.

My dad is the same way; he works so much (he's a fence contractor), and I tell him to just chill and relax! Like my mom, his meditation is working on cabinets or putting together some new house project (which I just get so frustrated by).

He enjoys a good doughnut in the morning with his coffee and sometimes a good ol' beer while sitting in his pool. I really like seeing my parents relax and laugh, enjoy a nice meal, and listen to some good tunes outside.

In January 2021, I took my parents and our doggies to Sedona, Arizona, and we went on hikes on the beautiful red rocks. My favorite hike was seeing the sun rise at the top of a mountain, and it was funny that they hiked up there with their doughnuts and coffees in hand.

Here are some different types of meditations that work for me. I try my best to get to them daily. I always ask myself first, "Which meditation do I need for today? Which will be the most helpful? Do I need to do some forgiveness today? Do I just need some quiet and presence? Do I need my brain to be more focused?"

COUNTING BREATHS MEDITATION

This helps me with focus and brings a nice calm. Maybe set the timer for five to ten minutes, and sit in a chair (I try the meditation pillows, but sometimes my ankles go to sleep or I start hunching my back). Focus on your breath, and each time you breathe out, count a number in your head. For example, "Breathe in, breathe out (1), breathe in, breathe out (2), breathe in, breathe out (3), breathe in, breathe out (4)." Then go back 4, 3, 2, 1, then forward 1, 2, 3, 4. Or you can go up to 8, then back to 1, then back to 8. You get it, yeah?

BREATHING MEDITATION

This one, trying to just focus on the breath, is the hardest for me. Thoughts arise, but then when you become aware that you are having a thought, just go back to focusing on the place in your body where the breath is the strongest. Is it your belly breathing in and out? Chest? Nostrils? Whichever part has the strongest sensation, just focus on that. Set a timer for five, ten, or more minutes. Start small and add time as you get better at it.

MEDITATION FOR SELF AND OTHERS

Jack Kornfield created a meditation called "loving-kindness meditation" and it's a meditation where you reflect on sending love and peace to people, animals, and yourself. See them in your mind and say kind words to them, anything you want! They can be "May you be filled with peace." "May you be so happy and healthy." And hey, you can do this for yourself too: "May I be joyful and kind."

My cat, Ella, the queen of meditation and naps.

Round of Applause

You know what feels good and can give you a good laugh for
the start of your day? When you wake up, just give yourself
a round of applause. Really clap and say, "Let's give it up for
_____ ; they woke up! Oh, hell yeah!!"

(your name)

Insecurities in the Cracks

Write your insecurities in these cracks. When you acknowledge them, you take away their power and see how silly they are.

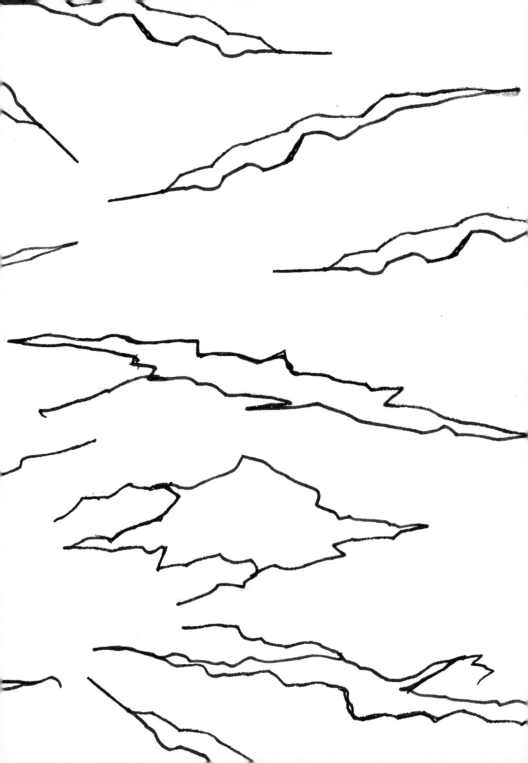

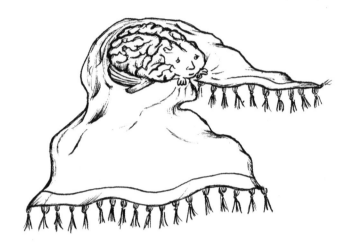

I started taking antidepressants in my mid-twenties when
I realized, *Oh, I'm really struggling with myself.* Confusing,
huh? Because I smile so damn much. Smiling is somewhat of
a people-pleasing mechanism, though. I exercised, I hung
out with family and friends, I did all the right things to help
get out of my clouds, but sometimes that wasn't enough.
Sometimes our brains don't have enough serotonin (happy
brain chemicals). I am nooooo medical professional here,
just sharing my experience! I am on Lexapro and Wellbutrin in
low dosages, and they help keep me in a good Melissa place.

Acceptance

I feel proud that I keep getting better at accepting me! It might be a superpower of mine. I think acceptance helps allow the silly comedy ideas to come out, and I feel so much more beautiful letting me be me. Sometimes when I have cat hair on my sweatshirt or bags under my eyes, I laugh about it and just accept it. I like to lean into and live my life by the maxim "funny and real is beautiful," not "being sexy and wearing lots of makeup is beautiful." (Don't get me wrong—when I doll up, ooh man, I look hot and can't look away from the mirror!) If I wake up and my hair is going in all different directions, I just say, "OK, hair! You lookin' like Edward Scissorhands? Great, let's be a weirdo today."

I think there must have been a seed planted in me in high school about accepting the weirdo within. At Ramona Convent Secondary School, an all-girls school, the teachers taught us that we are independent and free to be ourselves. I mean, no one said those exact words, but I just felt it being there. I showed up every day with messy, fluffy hair, braces, and overplucked eyebrows (my Gwen Stefani phase. I looked nothing like her, by the way. I looked more like the clown from *IT*), and I aimed to bring laughter.

e those flowers from someone special?
e those flowers from someone special?
e those flowers fro~ someone special?
those f~~~~~ someone special

th~o~~ ~~~~~ specia
t~~~se specia
th~s~ ~ia
th~~se spec

Yeah, me!

Accept Your Quirks

I am a freckle-faced gal. I didn't like it when I was little. I wish I didn't have any, but guess what? People wish they had freckles; they are unique and so pretty. When I was a teen, I was glad to find some thick-ass MAC foundation for my face, but it made me look like a pancake.

I still used foundation in my twenties, but I found foundation freedom in my thirties. I now never put on foundation. It's only applied if I am in the makeup chair. Sometimes I do put on some under-eye coverage because I genetically have pink-purple eye bags. I think I look like some cool Tim Burton character when they are noticeable, and I think I love it?

It's all internal too. There are days when I'm not wearing makeup and I look gorgeous and it's those days where I feel so good being me, and the glow just pours out from within my soul. I freakin' love those days, man!

Since I was very little, I've had a weak bladder, and I pee my pants if something makes me laugh hard. When I was younger, it was embarrassing if people found out I peed my pants. Thankfully, once I realized I was going to be a comedian, I owned my pee stuff. Don't worry, today it rarely happens. But hey, if it does, you're welcome for the hilarious memory.

Color this hair any color you want!

That's what is beautiful about being a comedian. I can make light of all the things I feel insecure about. This is partly why I love letting my gray hair grow—because it's so unique and so damn cool!

Gratitude

I enjoy making gratitude lists almost daily. (I try, guys, but it doesn't happen every day!) Gratitude can really shift the mind and help us appreciate how amazing the simple things we take for granted really are!

I mean, air conditioning! Water! Clean water to drink! Washing and drying machines to clean clothes! Sometimes if I am on the road for stand-up and a hotel doesn't have a laundry room, I just wash my clothes in the tub. I smile because handwashing makes me appreciate the clothes I have.

Sure, maybe I'm breaking, but I feel free.

Here are some of the things
I am grateful for today:

1. *I am grateful for the sun because it makes me feel joyful.*

2. *I am grateful for my parents being healthy and happy because that is the best gift to see.*

3. *I am grateful for my hair because it is thick and beautiful (thanks, Mom)!*

4. *I am grateful for the roof over my head. I'm also grateful for my head—it's nice to have one!*

5. *I am grateful for being healthy because I am able to run! And walk! And LIVE without physical pain. Right? Damn, gracias a dios.*

6. *I am grateful for having glasses/contacts because without them I can't see anything and would probably fall off a cliff.*

7. *I am grateful for my shoes because they keep my feet comfortable and moving.*

8. *I am grateful for having a front door and lock because if I didn't, anyone one could walk in, like a creepo or something that tries to kiss me.*

See, you can write the honest truth about the simple things you are grateful for and make yourself laugh while doing it!

_____

_____

_____

_____

_____

_____

_____

_____

_____

_____

Enjoy the
good while
it's good.

Hey, chill, will ya?
I love you.

ok.
My bad.

Read Something!

Here are some of the books I run to when I need to get back in a good mental place:

Daring Greatly
by Brené Brown

The Four Agreements
by Don Miguel Ruiz

Infinite Self
by Stuart Wilde

*The Subtle Art of Not Giving a F*ck*
by Mark Manson

The Untethered Soul
by Michael A. Singer

Also, any autobiographies of people I admire (a lot of comedians I adore)

Do Good and Help Others

One of the most important things about being an awesome person is doing good things for others. I believe I am a better me when my focus is on someone else, I'm helping others, and I'm doing some good for this planet. This is one of the big reasons why I do what I do. There's nothing like being able to connect with people and heal them (and bonus, I'm also healing myself!). This is my purpose, and I feel the most beautiful when my comedy and art come from my heart. At times, my ego gets wrapped up in it and wants approval and to be the best in the biz, but that isn't helping me or others. I always end up frustrated and alone when I do that. I have to pay attention and be mindful when I am doing my job so that it comes from a place of love.

Volunteer

I started volunteering in my early twenties while I was still living at my parents' house. I didn't get *SNL* the first time I auditioned in 2009, so I was heartbroken, broke, and lost. I dabbled in other things as I was floating around, not knowing what to do, thinking for sure that my dream was gone forever (so dramatic). I was becoming a big fan of nature and hiking trails, so in my hometown of Whittier, I joined this volunteer group, Puente Hills Habitat Preservation Authority, that helps preserve the trailheads in the city. We took local kids from schools on hikes to teach them about nature. Sometimes it wasn't fun. I would get pissed when I'd tell a kid some fun fact about trees, and meanwhile he'd point to an airplane and go "Cool!" I enjoyed (still enjoy) pulling weeds and planting trees. It felt nice because I was part of a community that was doing good for nature and humanity.

Whoops . . . I'm Awesome

What are some organizations you've volunteered for? If you haven't yet, it's OK! What things spark your interest that you might want to help with? Make a lil' list here.

_____

_____

_____

_____

_____

_____

_____

_____

_____

_____

Mail Letters

I began mailing letters recently because it's fun, man! I love writing a letter to a friend because you don't get an immediate response. You are, in a way, meditating and thinking about that person while writing, and you can let out your thoughts fully without interruption. I know that when a pal writes and mails me a fun card or note, I love seeing it in my mailbox—it can make my day. I enjoy putting stickers all over my notes and cards; it makes me laugh. Right now, I have stickers with *The Lego Movie* characters, dog paw prints, and gummy bears. One of my friends said her mom was looking through the mail, saw a card made out to her daughter, and thought some kid mailed it to her. Nope, it was just Meliss'!

I am trying to make a goal for Sunday to be the day I write letters. Or not even on Sunday, just whenever I need to step out of my own groove and place the attention on someone else. It feels great. I like writing funny things to friends like, "Penny's poo bag is like a little hand warmer in this twenty-degree weather in New York" or "My mom kicked my Nikes the other day and said, 'I hate these shoes of yours.'" Ha ha ha. Remember to write and share funny things with your friends and family. Write a letter here to someone and tell them why they brighten your day. Seriously—rip that page out and send it to them!

Call Someone

A day goes by so fast, and most of the time, we are in our own heads and that's creepy. Get the hell outta there every once in a while and call up some good pals.

For me, it's my cousin Caitlin, my aunt Lulie, my brothers and sister, and my sweet friends Sindie, Chelsea, Chase, Melody, and Matty.

Once I realized that the iMessage texting app had the option to send a voice text (it's the little microphone and you hold it while talking), I was pumped. I love being able to include voice inflections and emotions in my words, or else "Hi" can read as so damn cold. "Sup," "k," those words alone just suck.

Who are some people who, when you think of them, make you immediately smile? Immediately laugh?

_____

_____

_____

_____

_____

_____

_____

_____

_____

_____

Helping Friends

Once I moved into my LA place (first investment condo that my mom and aunt helped me with—they said it was a good adult step to invest, and I said OK!) during the summer of 2019, I began to meet and get to know my neighbors. One of my closest friends is my neighbor Terry. Terry is awesome, athletic, and has a beautiful house with a lot of colorful artifacts, art, and a sweet doggie named Kona. She is from Hawaii and definitely has Hawaiian style surrounding her and her spirit. I met her when our dogs met, and we just got along so well. She's kind and one of those folks who doesn't need a whole lot of input from my end as she chats; I can listen and learn and maybe at times zone out. She's cool because she does a lot of volunteer work for the city (food drives, phone banking, blood drives, etc.).

I soon began hanging out with her and sometimes helping her weed her front lawn. Weeding brings me down to earth (literally and metaphorically). Something about hands in soil is very powerful and makes me calm and quiet. It's a reminder that we are here on this planet. I am not great with plants, I'll be honest; I overwater or don't water enough or maybe give them too much light or too much darkness.

However, I did have some success in the summer of 2020. I planted geranium and sunflower seeds in a few pots, and two sunflowers bloomed. It was a win for me, and I was very proud. Cacti are more my plant, though, because they don't need much maintenance. They sort of remind me of me. I can be tough with spikes, basking in the sun to charge up, but every now and then, I must get water and grow some more.

Be proud of
your bright
light!

You Are My Sunshine

Sometimes we are the sun—happy, bright, and here for everyone. But sometimes we're drowing in a sea of it all. Who are some "suns" in your life that you reach out to for help? Who considers you their "sun"?

I got you.

Thank you.

Helping Family

My cousin Brandon started his own farm, Friendly Hills Farm, in our hometown of Whittier, California. He grows organic vegetables and fruits and has been having pop-ups in Uptown (which is our main street in Whittier).

I find that to be so cool and inspiring. He is an amazing chef and worked in fancy-schmancy restaurants from San Francisco to Los Angeles. Then he realized he wanted to go deeper and see where this food came from and how he could bring healthy and more delicious food to his community. Now, along with running the farm, he shares tips on fun meals to make with the ingredients he grows and caters when he pleases.

I do my best to visit his farm every time I go home to see how all his little babies have grown from sprouts and seedlings to beautiful, strong produce.

Color These Bugs!

Once, as a kid, I stepped on
a grasshopper with my bare
feet. Felt weird, but also,
sorry lil' dude!!

Gotta try to let go of
the who, when, and why,
and enjoy the ride.

Who?

When?

Why?

My sister is an actress, and I do what I can to help connect her with people I know in the biz. It makes me feel good to help her with headshots or clothes because I am fortunately now in a place where I can give and help. I have so much and my lil' sis is the cutest and I want the best for her in this world. I am grateful for my success and yes, I save, but I'd rather spend my money on others than myself.

My sis calls me her sugar mama, and I laugh and love it. I love taking care of her.

I went to work with my dad recently. He is a fence contractor in LA and puts up gates for homes and businesses. He works so hard, and I love when I have the opportunity and time to join him. I like to drive his truck and see him during his workday.

I accompanied him to my brother's house recently. He put a gate up there, and yeah, OK, I tried to drill some holes through these metal beams, and it was tough. I ended up taking a nap, but hey, I still went. I just have lil' lazy-ass hands. Even if I didn't get to work hard and sweat, it meant a lot and made his day just having me join him.

When I go out to eat with my parents, I always treat them, and they smile. I quote Jim Carrey's character, Lloyd Christmas, in *Dumb and Dumber,* and say, "There ya go! There ya go!" as Lloyd passes out stacks of cash when he pulls up in his Lamborghini at the hotel in Aspen.

As I get older, I realize that these are the only things that matter. Showing up for family and friends and laughing together and being present.

Donating

I donate to a few places at the moment. One of them is Planned Parenthood because, look, there has to be a safe place for women to get help. When I was a teen, I couldn't talk to my parents about sex, and my Catholic school didn't share much on it other than "DON'T DO IT," so I am grateful there's somewhere to go that exists for us. I donate monthly because there must be a place for women to not feel judged or shamed, because it can get scary, especially if you are alone in it.

I donate and volunteer with Treepeople, a organization in Los Angeles that helps many parks and trails in LA County. Last time I went, I helped by taking out old branches on a trail, I poured fresh mulch on the trail, and I used loppers to help trim a huge bush that was growing on the trail where people walked. My hands and arms were very, very sore the next day.

I'm continuing and always hope to continue my devotion to trees and nature because it's the place that brings me back to me when I feel like I'm losing myself. As I walk through the woods and along rivers and streams, my breathing is lighter and I smile more. Trails and nature must always exist for people to go to when they feel themselves drifting away. And, of course, ANIMALS! We must save land for the many animals that are on this planet; too many cities and towns have knocked down their homes. I applaud towns that have built animal crossings over highways so they can stop getting hit by dumb cars.

Another awesome organization that I have been recently volunteering for and donating to is Feed the Streets LA. It wakes me up and puts things in perspective. A couple times every week people can volunteer to serve coffee and donuts at 7 am at Skid Row. There's something quiet, special, and peaceful early in the morning. There's no judgment of stuff coming from my brain. I'm learning and see so clearly how damn fortunate I am. They are a great organization and always can use the helping hand. If you feel that you have got the goods and time to help others in need, come join me.

A tiny gardener can create big, beautiful things.

PENNY

I adopted my dog, Penny, from Best Friends Animal Society, and she really is my best friend. Adopting her was one of the best decisions I ever made. I love her to pieces, and she feels like she's a part of my body, if that makes any sense. She protects me and makes me laugh and brings me comfort when I've had a long day. She gets me outside and makes me stop to stare at a leaf or a flower.

Best Friends is a great organization to get your new best friend from, and there are many others too. I sometimes stumble onto a post online of doggies that need help with surgery or medicine, and I immediately donate. I love animals so much. And yeah, I am that girl who will cry more for an animal dying in a movie than a human.

I'm all over the place but you keep me here smiling, warm, and safe.

Hey, you deserve some serious dog love.
Draw yourself among this fluffy little guys
and soak in the love.

Hey
there . . .

I hope you've enjoyed this book and can lean on it
in moments when you need a friend or to recenter
yourself. I appreciate you being here and hope
you go forth on your journey with silliness, good
health, light thinking, and love. You are awesome!

Acknowledgments

I am truly thankful to so many people in my life that believed in me to get this book done!

First off one of my best friends/my manager Tatiana! You never give up on me even in those moments where I've completely given up on myself. Thanks for being patient with me on the days when my ego swirls into a tornado. To my whole team at WME for being so badass and waiting on no one. Thank you for being freakin' badasses.

My family! Thank you to Mom and Dad for enjoying everything I create even if it's dark. I love you so much! My sister Ally, your smile and heart can warm me up any time I see you or even think of you. Michael and Andrew, my brothers who make me laugh and always teach me beautiful, wise things—you are always looking out for me. I couldn't have made it anywhere without all of my family. You are the best. Curly, my cousin, for connecting so much with my art. I always wanna be like you, Cait, you light up any room. Lulie, thank you for encouraging me to keep going no matter the pain. I love our chats on art and life and spiritual things.

My dear friend Heidi Gardner for always being moved by my art and always sharing it. You are a star, Heidi, and one of the best hearts I know!

My dear talented friend Melody, my sister since high school. I love how we can get to that peace on our art days and thanks for always living that cozy life with me.

Thank you to my therapist J for always reminding me that I'm enough and for being that voice in my head that I can hear when I need the right soothing things to tell myself.

Thank you to my angels and the universe for always having my back and knowing the best timing for me in my journey. How do you always know?!

Thank you to Lorne and everyone at *Saturday Night Live* for opening this big door in my life to opportunities and for providing so many gifts beyond what I could even imagine.

Thanks to all the hotels that I stayed in and cried in on the road after bombing stand-up shows, because you were the seed of inspiration for me to draw.

AND! Don't worry, Meliss' didn't forget about YOU!! My fans! You are rockstars. Damn, I am so grateful for you. For laughing with me, for coming to my shows, and for supporting me through the years. Thank you for connecting with this sensitive side of me and for helping me not feel alone in my feelings. It's so special to see the art account and its fans grow throughout the years.

Buckets of joy and smiles,